CANTILEVERED
songs

CANTILEVERED
songs

JOHN LENT

03/11/09
For Liz,
All the best in your
work for all of on.

John

thistledown press

Thistledown Press Ltd.
633 Main Street
Saskatoon, Saskatchewan, S7H 0J8
www.thistledownpress.com

Library and Archives Canada Cataloguing in Publication

Lent, John
Cantilevered songs / John Lent.

Poems.
ISBN 978-1-897235-66-9

I. Title.

PS8573.E58C45 2009   C811'.54   C2009-904216-9

Cover and book design by Jackie Forrie
Printed and bound in Canada

Mixed Sources
Cert no. SW-COC-001271
© 1996 FSC
FSC

Thistledown Press gratefully acknowledges the financial assistance of the Canada Council for the Arts, the Saskatchewan Arts Board, and the Government of Canada through the Book Publishing Industry Development Program for its publishing program.

 Canada Council
for the Arts
Conseil des Arts
du Canada
 SASKATCHEWAN
ARTS BOARD
 Canadian
Heritage
Patrimoine
canadien

Acknowledgements

The writer wishes to thank all his writing students and colleagues at Okanagan College for being so supportive and encouraging.

"Weightless" and "Light" are dedicated to Mary Ellen Holland; "August Dream" and "Racoon" are dedicated to Craig McLuckie; "Variations: Brothers" is dedicated to Tim Lent, and "Snow" to my mother, Adrienne Winifred Lent.

I need to thank the following for being so specific in their support and friendship: Mary Ellen Holland; Dennis Cooley; Robert Kroetsch; Betty Clarke; Ross Tyner; Glen Sorestad; Ron and Doreen McLuckie; Kevin McPherson; Phil Lambert; Don Summerhayes; George Larsen; Virginia Dansereau; Greg Simison; Harry, Susan, and Tim Lent; Al Forrie; Jackie Forrie; and, John Murphy.

Neil Fraser and Shelby Wall are a big part of the rhythm and the heart of this collection, and I know my singing is dependent upon them.

Craig McLuckie has been my friend and gauge throughout.

Okanagan College has been the greatest place to teach that I know of.

Thanks to Jude Clarke, my wife, who has created a life for me that is supportive, private, and filled with her own artistic vision which I draw on constantly.

Finally, my thanks to Susan Musgrave who took a sprawling manuscript and got me to tighten up and focus the music in ways I could not see or hear.

for my mentor, Don Summerhayes

Contents

11   Weightless

12   Gabrielle, Jumping for Joy

14   August Dream

17   Taking Jude Out For Breakfast
On A Sunny Spring Sunday In Summerland, Thirty Years After God

19   Your Body As Fall Breeze

22   Molecular Cathedral

24   Carpenter

26   Morning Walk Backwards

28   The Racoon

30   Home

32   I must lie down where . . .

35   Intersections

38   Portillo's

39   The Creek

40   Spring, thinking of leaving

42   Ryga's Window

44   Carbon

45   Listening To Lightfoot On The Highway

46   Trees

47   Heat

50   The Martyr

52   The Peanut Crunching Crowd

53   Watching My Students Write An Exam On Wilderness

55   Bill Evans and this sky today

57   Variations: brothers

61   Light

63   Snow

66   Thinking of First Meeting Don Coles in 1971

67   Winter Blues

69   Dog in a Half-Ton Sun

On these walks he began to understand how the two planes fused, as his world of imaginary marvels was embedded in the ordinary: the bells of sheep, the minor-key songs of women floating disembodied through the air, even the sudden, unexpected appearance of a visiting film company in the midst of this sunbaked, isolated landscape.

— Eileen Warburton, *John Fowles: A Life In Two Worlds* (2004)

... we lack the cognitive maps that would allow us to position ourselves in this world, to know where we are. This is true not only on the level of shared or public life. Our interior lives have become equally disoriented. [...] the aim [...], then, is to start to redraw the cognitive maps ...

— Nick Mansfield, *Subjectivity: Theories Of The Self From Freud to Haraway* (2000)

Home, we may say, is the action of the inner life finding outer form; it is the settling of self into the world [...] It turns wilderness into an interior and presents interiority to the wilderness.

— Don Mckay, *Vis a Vis* (2001)

WEIGHTLESS

I drive around the city like everybody else. I clean out the side-compartments
in the dark crevices and seams of the door of my car where I crumple up chocolate
bar wrappers and stuff them sometimes. On other days I can get organized
enough to wash and vacuum the whole thing creating a brand new world
of car in an hour. And I walk on the cement sidewalks in my sandals
and feel the heat of these sunny spring days through the leather and through
my exposed toes. I walk past the enamel-painted frames of the windows
leading into my favourite café and order the usual the usual the usual,
lugging my take-out coffee onto the charcoal streets, squinting
into the afternoon sun, gripping the steering wheel with real
hands, real flesh, drop by the bank, take some money out, pay some
bills, put some money in, all the usual stuff, all the usual stuff,
and drive up onto the shaded asphalt of my own driveway, turn
the car off, breathe in the heavy tree-scented air, see the lush
gardens she has made, feel the wood of the gate as it creaks
open, reach down to look into the eyes of my loyal dog who
loves me, sense myself anchored in all this, and walking
through my back door into my home where everything
sits where it's supposed to, heavily and solemnly as my
life, I feel myself begin to thin out in the world, through
the ceiling of my solid house, away from the heart's
gravity, and up over the grey-shingled roof that
covers and protects everything I love, and into
these blue skies (which aren't really blue when
you're ascending, but hard to nail down, hard
to describe), now substance-less in an ether
you're examining, so far away from
my care . . . *throw me back*, I gasp,
throw me back . . . unhook me from
this eerie other element and heave
me back down there where I can
swim and love and turn into a dust
that doesn't frighten me.

GABRIELLE, JUMPING FOR JOY

Don't know where this one's going to go, but I saw my niece Gabrielle last night
on the landing between the stairs, excited about driving down from Edmonton, thrilled
to be visiting here, be on her way downstairs to the sliding glass doors where
she knew the pool was waiting. After she'd given me the obligatory hug
and smile, had answered a few meaningless questions about the drive
and how long it had been, she looked away, her eyes glazed over
in abstraction, and jumped up involuntarily, into the height
of the air above the landing where you could go up or down,
lifted herself off the ground, her arms wrapped tightly
around her small, eleven year old frame — right into
the air — and in the middle of this ecstasy,
in the fractions of its ascent and descent, our eyes
locked in a distance that is not necessarily
the same world we think it is and I
was happy to have been
there to see her
and be dragged
by her into this
fiercer world
we sometimes
forget to find,
even though
it is at
the heart
of the one
we see.

Driving down the asphalt later, the soft swooshing sounds
of summer everywhere around me like water in the indigo air, the florescent lights
of the gas station flickering like fish into the streaks of imperfection
on my night windshield, and the muffled, sliding sounds of skateboards
on the concrete loops in Polson Park playing a staccato polyrhythm
to my heart, stones on the bottom pulsing against the water
above them, I kept seeing Gabrielle on the staircase,
suspended between going up
and going down, an incarnation
of fins and water.

AUGUST DREAM

Maybe because it's half-way through summer and certain subterranean fall anxieties
start to sift into my evening dreams, and the caterwauling chunky charcoal dreams
of summer, though still smiling, begin to cringe in the hallway, slightly
offstage but always insistent, I woke up at 3:00am
in the middle of a complex dream that ended up with me singing
"Silent Night" to a young woman down in the dark
alleys off Leith Way in Edinburgh — my voice never more
full and rich than when I was singing the line, "Christ
Our Saviour Was Born," all eerie and twisted,
considering — so I sat stunned in the dark
for a while, trying to remember the odd
and lumpy logic of everything happening
in that other world I seemed to live in,
too.

In the dream I was in Edinburgh with my best friend, Craig, who is Scottish
by birth, born in Falkirk, raised in Livingston, *and the thing is*, Jude and I
lived in Edinburgh in 1994 when Craig was living in Sterling, so we'd
been in the city at the same time and maybe that added weight
to the chalky, damp texture of the dream, the cobblestone sidewalks
and the heavy, practical clothes and the bright enamel colors,
I'm not sure, but there you go. It was the emotional
landscape of the dream that drew me in, caused
a rush of sadness that was so heavy
I woke myself up weeping.

The people in the dream were close to Craig, like his parents. In fact, maybe
they *were* his parents but if they were they were living back in Scotland instead
of St. Albert where they live now. Things were going wrong with the family
in the dream, as in a James Kelman vision of everyone meaning well
but getting hurt anyway, each person withdrawing into that hurt,
cloistered in small airless rooms or stairwells.

In one part of the dream, for example, Craig and my good intentions
accidentally prompt Craig's Mom to quit her job as a Social Worker
because of our exuberant left-wing views and the fallout of her
decision does not go over well with the rest of Craig's family.
Just when I think there's a possibility of the quiet rifts
being mended, Craig disappears on a bender and I
can't find him anywhere. I'm looking for him
everywhere in Edinburgh, down all its
streets and paths.

It's night and I'm lost and I know that our failure to show up somewhere
is going to cause wider rifts in this dream family, so it matters
to me that I find him. Out of the darkness of these streets,
morning must have arrived for color begins to fill the dream
and this pretty girl is backing away from me — the camera
angle is my eyes now . . . I *am* the camera — and she's
backing away from me and I know she's jittery and anxious
and paranoid, and I realize she's a junkie and she's afraid
of me, but in the dream I can't see myself now because I *am*
the point of view of the dream and I'd need a mirror
to see what I look like so I stretch out my hands
and they're clown's hands and I begin to suspect
I appear as a bloated, robust Falstaff,
stretching exaggerated hands out
to her and I am aware, too, that I am
singing to her, I am singing
"Silent Night" to her
and part of me is surprised
and even struggles a bit
wondering if this isn't
some crazy secularization
of my past life growing up

as a Catholic,
but there I am, in full voice,
enunciating that final phrase
with all its emphases:
"Christ Our Saviour
Was Born . . ."

. . . and I turn away from the girl and twenty children swarm me, giggling
and laughing, their voices small birds in the morning air, and I realize I am a gigantic
presence to them, an emblem or myth of fun and laughter, and as I turn down
yet another alley with these children following me, I spot Craig up ahead.
It's morning now and he gives me this rueful nod, apologizing for the
night before, and I smile back and watch as my red clown hand
stretches out for a smoke and the dream ends
with Craig and I trying to figure out how to mend
all the sadness in the city around us in the morning light
and the infinity of that sadness makes me weep
in front of Craig for all this darkness
that won't go away . . .

Taking Jude Out For Breakfast
On A Sunny Spring Sunday In Summerland, Thirty Years After God

O God of my lost Catholic childhood, hiding in whatever dark corner of those edgy
years I flung myself into so flatly out there on my sidewalks it's a wonder
there's anything *left*, and even knowing you will never assume the form you
once had in my smiling, earnest years, a trust just above the freckles and loose grin,
and admitting my world transformed into *this one here*, the one I'm in now, the one
my body loves, and though I never did this body any favours — even so — I still
think of a wheel of time, the revolution on those clanging, dusty Edmonton
streets, hustling across Whyte Avenue in a February wind, swanning
into Uncle Albert's Pancake House — before franchises, before enclosed
shopping malls — our first introduction to sophistication maybe (we thought),
going out to a restaurant on a Sunday morning, Christine clutching my left
hand, our faces fresh from Mass at St. Joseph's Chapel on the campus,
Father Pendergast in full, soft flight behind us now, the two of us mincing
along Whyte Avenue in a cool wind, as young as we would ever be, our
bodies slim willows moist in a vague pre-spring it seems looking back
now, our shadows cast in front of us on the pale cement,
us trying to interpret those forms dancing in front of us against
the grey, who those people might become in their lives, dark kisses
stretching before us, back-lit by a Catholic God above
and behind us whose long fingers spun fragile threads
connected to our hearts, and shortly to be severed as we
would spin alternately away from both our selves
and that soil we'd been planted in, away into this
room here, its white walls, its peace, even its loony
longing to return to those streets sometimes, but
its firm smile that *this* is enough, *this* its own vertical
light, no strings, no fingers, just a heart beating
in a dark it can take most of the time —
but even so, O God of my long lost
Catholic childhood, *listen:*

lift off the layers of hate that descend
upon us like cages, lift this sour angry light
off the streets so there is no shadow, so
we walk in a flat, translucent dignity
over streets of gold, then re-
turn to the moist, dark soil
we came from, the real soil,
enough.

YOUR BODY AS FALL BREEZE

This morning, walking the Grey Ditch Canal
above the town, the long red clay paths
of trampled couchgrass, a guiltwalk really. We
knew that from the start: our neglected Lhasa
Apso, Finnegan, hadn't been out
for a run in at least four days, had been
eyeing us sideways for the last two, thinking
thoughts we didn't want to know about
her, about us really. So we got up in that
guilt and rattled round the house, more
buoyant than usual, suspiciously
confident because we *knew* we had
this walk planned, though *she* didn't.
It was funny at first to see
the despondency she'd grown so used to
give way to her innocence as I
rooted out my running shoes
and she heard you getting
ready in the bathroom until
it clicked for her and her
body shuddered
in an ecstasy of anticipation,
and she forgave us,
and, at least for now,
stared into my
eyes the way
you used to.

                    Up on the hill,
at the walk's entrance, I hear the doors
of our Echo close and snicker behind us
like creases in clothes, a soft that's-the-way-

things-always-work-when-they're-new-and-still-
solid-and-fresh kind of noise, when everything
fits into everything else, and all that fitting
is enabled in a mathematical seam of fresh,
untried, snugness of surface on surface.
nothing like it.

But we leave these perfect
noises behind and enter the wild trail and all
the humid, cool, grey mist and fog
that has collected above the town. Usually,
we can, at a certain height on this path,
stare down at Vernon splaying herself out
brazenly among three lakes, at the moist centre
of three mountain valleys, water coming from
all directions, pooling below where we stand
for thousands of years.

Finnegan runs ahead, stopping
occasionally to make sure we're watching,
heaving her tiny black nose into any small
shrub or scent of berries, pee, fur, grass,
dirt, shit. It's all a feast to her, and some
clownish chrome tumbler rolls and clicks
in the tarnished steel lock assemblages
I conceal myself in at how she commits
herself to the present, the microscopic
texture of what is, an infinity to her
finite, wet nose, her sight so
much wider than mine.

I imagine my snug self
running ahead of her's, scuttling into every
crevice and hollow, following my nose
into the darkest, most moist seam
here, instinctive, my eyes
wild with *now*. And I imagine
you waiting for the ambulance
to pull up to retrieve me, sedate
the very thing we admire in our
dog, and it makes me wonder
how we pretend not to *have* our
noses and eyes, how we forget
the breath of our skin at least,
the open joy of that skein,
the scent of it, the musky
re-creation.

Then I see you
walking next to me, the membrane
you are, the fissures, your rustling
silk skin against the field of my
cheek, the stretches of you fading
into distance, your scent
everywhere you are
endless.

Molecular Cathedral

This was the poem I didn't want to write, the scary poem that insists
self-interest is the origin for each human action and you have to either
acknowledge that or you're in big trouble and, of course, we don't want
to admit this might be true; we've got way better stories to tell, movies
to make, tearful TV specials to watch on slow Monday evenings
in the fall — but *there ya go!* It's like reading Richard Ford's *Wildlife*
or Celine or Vonnegut on certain days and then trying
to go about living a normal life knowing most of our narratives
of normal are only wild dreams of neo-platonic perfects
selling us the very world our selfishness thinks
it needs to protect and destroy itself at the same
strange time: a bloodied intersection we're
left standing in, the crossroads Robert Johnson
sings about, where we are both consuming
and consumed. *Holy Crap!*

This is the poem I dream about at night restless in my half-sleep,
full of guilt and self-loathing, the poem that saves me from myself,
blesses me with some alternative, whispers redemption into my left
ear while a right hand hovers above my forehead with holy
oil to anoint me so I can get up and walk into the day
with an innocence I might not otherwise find.
It's a dream of primal connection where eyes
look on me with love and forgive me everything.

So how does the poem settle its own tensions and oppositions?
How can the poem resolve selfishness and connection to others
and the brutal green limits that gird these fields of time and matter? How can
we accept this vessel of flesh and bone, this home, and not destroy it and allow
it to turn in a bright field of other dancing bodies, occasionally intersecting, touching,
alive in a primal *presence* and a longing past safety and hunger, for replication, yes,
but for something more, too, something not anticipated maybe, always a surprise,

something that moves us past our selves in a whoosh of logic we cannot
see or sense until we are standing there, unaccommodated
in an open field, staring both at the intricate web of skin
on our hands and the blue, blue air of summer we're gulping
down like water against the heat, this incarnation we are,
the word made flesh, a molecular cathedral straining
within itself, its medieval, gothic balances
and counter-turns and arches and cross-bracing,
its unimaginable architecture a gift
that *requires* selfishness as a *pledge* not
a betrayal of love: the harder
path even.

CARPENTER

The finches, chickadees and wrens have wildly returned this morning
in the bird feeder outside our front window. I repaired it yesterday. The birds
had worn it out over the winter so it was teetering
to the rhythm of their pecking, and threatening to fall beneath
their weight and the shifting weight of the snow and rain as well.
I took a few hours and found some old 3/4" slats and cast-
away 3/8" plywood.

                    I began drawing what I imagined
I needed on a piece of paper. This is always a good move for me
as it discloses, early on, mistakes in logic and architecture
I will invariably make. By drawing it out, I visualize precisely what
I'm trying to do and anticipate errors by seeing through the sketch
to the real. *Always interesting when you look back on it.* And it all
worked out, this small making. I'm pleased. The birds seem
happy.

                    But I find myself standing
on the lawn now, staring at this thing I've made, amazed, and another
version of me standing even further back, watching the first,
is muttering, laughing: *yes, it's amazing, for you've made some
thing out of the stuff of this world, and you have, for once,
joined it perfectly.* And there it is again, this mystery
of joining, of intersections, corners, fits, so
damn important in everything we do, each
small jazz symphony we might
construct, for example,

or song we might want
to sing in the middle
of a night, or poem
to the earth, our dust,
or this thought
here, or this
join and
hinge:
you.

MORNING WALK BACKWARDS
For Ron Grainge

I'm doubling back down the street a bit earlier this morning so the world I enter
is a world occurring twenty minutes *before* the world I entered yesterday. Twenty
minutes and it's changed, every bit of it. That's just how volatile these parts
and elements and moveable gears and levers can be in the light and the dark
as we stumble by them or into them or even when we collapse and wrap them
around ourselves when we cannot bear any more movement, any more
change, and it makes me think of the lost ones, the *disappeared* who
grew up in our neighbourhoods on the southside of Edmonton back
then, ran down the lanes with us, stared up at the power poles during
football games and gulped the same air and scrounged for pop
and rides in the summer and hoped for many things, all of us boys
eyeing up the girls from the other schools — us being
mysterious to these girls, so obvious to our own —
hanging out at The Chinese Grocery drooling
over the penny candy, plopping our bikes down
on the smooth lawn off Saskatchewan Drive, stretching
out on the fresh cut summer grass, staring at the fat
brown river below, the myth coursing through
our childhoods, the true length of our bodies, just
lying there yacking, before there were shopping
malls, before everything got processed, before
it all got weird: those great eyes you
had, Ron, your easy laugh, your
freckled good looks and will,
your difficult, early exit
from all this, your death

a soft chill in a hallway,
performed on the sidelines
of something else, only
caught by the corner
of an eye maybe, only
registered in a wistful
sideways comment
years later, what
a loss of you my
friend, what
a fault in the
air you dis-
appeared
into.

Back then we didn't have the language to bring you back
or comfort ourselves even. We accepted the swish of a door closing
quietly, never talked about, never mourned, your death.

We loved you and our arms encircle you even there
wherever there is and whatever time might be
we think of you and hope you will
get back to us here
in time.

The Racoon

It's spring and I have a new family of sparrows
in the birdhouse. Last year, just after the babies were born,
about a week after, a racoon climbed up the Manitoba maple
in the middle of the night, stretched its cunning paws
into the tiny opening — paws that look so like human hands —
then killed the parents by feel, by trapping them in the dark,
shook the birdhouse out, and scampered down
the trunk to finish off the baby birds who couldn't, of course,
fly. In the morning, all I found on the deck were
the straw-strewn feathered remains of all five
abandoned near the garbage can.

The act seemed astonishing to me. I know it
shouldn't have, but that doesn't matter. It did.
I kept thinking of this small family, those prying black
fingers and furtive eyes, and an acceptance,
somewhere in there, that all was lost.

Their chittering through the leaves when they'd
first shown up, the purposeful gathering of twigs
and string to feather the nest, then the seclusion
of the hen, and finally, in time, Jude and I smiling like
idiots through the glass of our kitchen window
from where we could see the three tiny open
mouths cawing relentlessly for food.

Of course, there was something unprotected
in the field of this imagery, something devastating,
that bothered me . . . *Come and get me you sly, dark*
heaving motherfucking shit-stuffed prick,
just try to ruin all this take it all away, I'll
fucking kill you going down with you,
you miserable old toothless hag, you
bloated civil servant mandarin, you
fucking piece of endlessly patronizing,
supposedly superior authority, I'll
show you what you deserve you
piece of shit . . . and reminded me of things
in my own life whatever they may be.

. . . OK, I've been waiting for the racoon all
my life . . .

Home

*No doubt the Indians came here not only for water but also, from time to
time, to camp and hunt. For the Indians this was not a remote hideaway
in a wilderness but an extension of their home; for them the wilderness
was home.*

— Edward Abbey, "A Walk in the Desert Hills," in *Beyond the Wall*

Cafeterias in hospitals, in shopping malls sometimes,
though the ones in malls tend to be called names like Food Courts
or Towne Centres or Village Greens, funny if you think
about those words for a while. Funny if you think
of the word 'home' at the same time. How we feel that
word, how we imagine what it refers to, how we
use its idea as a redemptive chorus whispering over
any other place we might get lost in, or frightened in.
Any wood. My comfort in these artificial 'homes'
is a destination, though, and that's the tricky issue: I have
surfaced out of the water and walked up onto
a shore that was arduously sought for. Prices were
paid to deliver me here. I have these voices in my
blood that sang me sitting here, dreamed by leaving
homeland behind, forsaking it even, in two or three
hundred years descendants might become the freedom
to live out a wilderness, here, the one you can't
see even, the one that keeps me so stumped
in its contours and blinds and cul-de-sacs,
and which opens up for miles and simply
miles of a thick, green, moist confusion,
another kind of everything.

And I accept its rootlessness
as an ache that will not retreat and gnaws
at the edges of movement and side-
ways glances; as difficult as it might be,
I accept its shifting, crazy balancing
act in the names of the blood that
dreamed me. This wilderness is
my home.

And the vertigo? A good thing
in many ways, to be often off-
balanced by these textures
and this light, the wild neon forest
of its tangled intersections I end up
caught in: when I stare *out*
and *in* at exactly the same time
and feel it finally, and arrive feet
flat on the gravel, nose in
the pines, eyes on the blue,
blue lungs heaving in
then out, showing up
here at dusk say,

burning.

Hybrid.

I MUST LIE DOWN WHERE . . .

O the long thin dark corridor opening out
onto these blue fields, so we get, almost
instantly, a vertigo cradle of *in* and
out, enclosed and unenclosed, dark and
light — ourselves, of course — and we
see ourselves moving out and back in,
over and over, as in Yeats' Noh play
"Purgatory," sense those selves most
intensely in the borders where such
shuffling occurs, and where a great
ruckus clacks within the smooth
but intricate joining and
slippage of this loom.

>   (The thing is, *the thing is this*: if we
>   choose one or the other, or, if we
>   choose one or the other *and* lament
>   the swinging back and forth, and would
>   prefer, even, to occupy just one *or*
>   the other completely — as immanence — we
>   make a mistake that cannot be undone
>   easily, and we assume a lifetime
>   of longing for the one thing that cannot
>   *be*, the one thing that will elude us,
>   while another kind of joy, another
>   kind of immanence slips past too,
>   slips past because we are obviously
>   not looking for it . . . ah . . .)

. . . and you are running. You see
your naked feet swing out beneath the rest
of your flesh, registering the morning
dew that slips and sifts in the dark
tendrils of long green brome beneath
you and you squint through this mist,
against this soft spring rain, to see how
vast and unending the field is
and as you're nodding to yourself,
as you begin to inhale the green
endlessness before you, and the animal
muscle naturalness of it — the giddy glee
of being there as a rough red body
full of moisture too — just as you are
choosing this field and this body,
you are clothed in silk
and find yourself walking down
an austere corridor that spits you
out into the bottom
of an intricate, bound cathedral
made of oak, and it both rises above
you in cross-beams and subtle
joinery and whirls around
you in patterns you only begin
to understand, and you run your hand
against and into seemingly seam-
less joining and you fall in love
with the still supple architecture

of this kind of movement, its thick,
cerebral stillness,
and at the instant of your acceptance
of it, as you are yourself convinced
of its relieving solidity, you're
back in this field again, here, now,
running against the sun and moon
in the gauze-strewn blue air
of the heart . . .

INTERSECTIONS

1.

It's what you begin to see as you grow older and it's not
that it's a surprise. Standing, having a smoke in the gravel
parking lot of a truck-stop in Merrit, you remember sifting
through the bookstore offerings earlier, back in Vancouver,
registering the obvious glare of new voices, new techniques,
other generations whispering up behind yours, and you had
to accept the seduction was already *over*, past you, and any
of your pronouncements about the lure of fame and glory
were, in fact, precisely accurate: your voice was *not* going
to announce itself, or even whisper, or if whispering,
it was going to be the tiny swoosh of a wren or a sparrow
flitting past your head in this truck-stop, the sound of pines
creaking like looms in the wind, *that* subtle, *that* soft, *that* in-
tricate really, or a saxophone reeling back into its improvised
maelstrom of gravity in the middle of a piece, stretching
and winging away into the inside of the wind, the ear of the bird,
the heart of the pine.
                            That you are here as planted
and as green as everything else: *that* is the gift itself, *that*
communion of air, of earth, of water. Fire in your head
as raging — as bill bissett would say — as raging as the ear
of the wind, the heart of the bird, the inside of the pine, all
one and raging in an inarticulate rush of breath and pulse
and fibre, immediate, immanent, all old testament god stirring
on gravel, slouching, ready, there, the bellows of the lungs meshed
through the cortex to the lips to the reed, all the deep, fluted,
sharp bird and wind and pine notes flapping into the air
as themselves, as hymn to the nothing-really-matters-but-this-
moment-now song, being *in* it, being.
                                          Your body
pivots over the rough, pebbly asphalt, the wind creases

and folds as air, the long stretches of bird and pine
and sage fall away in intersecting planes of matter and you've
been deposited as Adam in this creaking, folding, billowing,
crazy and imperfect paradise, standing squarely, singing
through the lips of Eden.

2.

the care-
ful turn-
ing turn-
ing turn
of tongue
and pa-
lette and
grunt and
groan of
words that
need to
try to say
what it
is, having
to take a
picture of
the pic-
ture of
the picnic
more than
having the
picnic it-
self: that
fear that

forces us
to arrest
it while
it's mov-
ing. Let it
be. *Don't.*
Don't!

3.

did you give your care
to something else? Your focus
and attention? Did you
forget your self?

4.

the tree the bird the wind
and you there, too, your in-
drawn wilderness accelerating
into the other, two songs
one song until the black, dark,
charcoal silence of the earth in which,
on which, other equal songs
braid the sweet-sweet marbled
clay and air and water: combustion
engine everywhere aflame until
all weaving ends in light

5.

Play that song.
Play it again.
Now, *improvise.*

PORTILLO'S

Haven't written for so long I'm worried
I've forgotten every slant every note
and it's all evanesced into the air like
water in my head 'cause I'll soon be
dead and all the urgent senses that things
matter are shifting like harsh illusions through
and inside and down and up the length
of the body of my mind.

Didn't think it *had* a body
for the longest time until I saw through time
itself and saw its body turn
to gauze to mist and slight rain
on asphalt on the edge
of a town, beyond the sounds
and the morning voices
and coughing of engines and doors
and railroad cars in the chafing
wind off the ocean: here again

on this small height above
and beyond this small town I never
moved to and never lived in
but *do* live in *here*, now,

this body sitting here is also there
on that small bluff, a body
in time, through time, sideways
in the universe and in love

with every moving thing, alive.

The Creek

The water looks so clear, and there isn't too much refuse
even on the sidebanks, so you can see the bottom everywhere
you look, and the translucent catfish hovering in the middle,
poised over food of some kind, insects, plants, I'm not sure,
and the slow clear flow of the water from one large lake to another so
the creek bisects this city sitting between two lakes
and has this quiet ribbon of clear blue water sifting through
its middle like emotions we sometimes savour, matters we don't
announce to other people, thoughts dancing in and out of
the sunlight and populated with tenacious growth,
especially on the sides of thoughts, and sometimes, big
grey catfish grinning in dreams and lean and lucid
trout racing through a sluice of rushes of water and plants
almost as fast and as silver as light itself, almost
as temporary as understanding, so beautiful,
then gone, leaving us standing
in the afterimage of clarity,
on an asphalt covered parking lot
staring into water, looking
my whole life long
at water connecting
deep blue
bowls
of me.

SPRING, THINKING OF LEAVING

Dusk in spring Sonny Rollins
a match for the fragrances out there
in the yard aching in bud and blossom, every
thing cracking itself out and open and back
into the thick of the world, the musk of it, so everything
is simply happening, blowing, and we're rolling,
a part of it and we're improvising too, but like
the green we too seem to have some
celestial code chipped into our system
somewhere . . . we too seem to be moving
forward all right, as if we knew what
we were doing when we know
we don't . . . and the hilarious thing
in a way . . . maybe the price of the fall
of humankind . . . that we roll forward in
this heaven here, not recognizing it at all,
deferring it in fact, and are the only living
species in this whole green ecstasy that
is suspicious, self-conscious, guilty,
clever, triple-thinking its way
through
the universe.

Would we have it any other way?

Have we ever had it any other way?

We are the unexpected guest
at the feast and it's all we ever
talk about in the sinew
of the muscle of the contraction
and expansion of green silk

dreams of green silk twining
in a real world we cannot
see or breathe until we're
so frightened of leaving
it we finally blink and
there it is by gum our
grail, emptying, Rollins
fading into the coda
behind me, of course,
always behind.

Ryga's Window

What *is* it about the quiet ones,
their hushed power and the risk
that it will never prevail? What *is*
it about the gentle-voiced men
and women, crowded together
in the modesty of not-being-sure-of-anything,
of being-at-the-mercy-of, going about their
rich, leaved lives, blossoming in self-
deprecating smiles, shy entrances
and exits?

In contrast, of course, to the endless,
straining, painful mediocrity
of the noisy ones, the pushy ones, the in-
secure loud-mouthed ones who want
to simplify the world so they can
stuff it up their asses in the name
of *Jesus*, of the common good,
of democracy, or global *something*
or whatever other drain has claimed
the short-lived grab of their noisy,
stumbling greed.

The only hope we have
is in the whispered love of the quiet ones;
even the noisy ones know this
when they scare themselves.

It's always been like this I suppose.
It's likely never been any different.
I've lived just long enough to know.

Praise the gentle, soft-voiced humans
for they shall inherit what is left
of this earth's collapsing acceleration.

Praise them and whisper back:
It's going to be all right.
Everything's going to be all right in the end
because of you.

. . . and a fat spring robin lands
in the birdbath outside George Ryga's
kitchen window, Rita Joe come back
singing, rising up out of the quiet
to sing us to sleep in the middle
of a hot afternoon, the orchards blooming
this weekend, the Oregon grape
stalks crazy in a waxen yellow
kiss, the Saskatoon vines a pale
lace veiling and unveiling this
valley in a delicate, shy hope.

CARBON

Rain rinses the green and red fauvist street outside the window,
while birdsong becomes a second envelope in the moist grey chalk
kiss, and Coltrane the third membrane pulsing beneath these other
skins. I'm sitting here wondering, hitting the keyboard every now
and then, the nature of my species dawning on me slowly, like being
hit over the head by the forest *and* the trees: that our gift,
our stewardship, is to bear witness to these skins as well as
receiving them, the vehicle of attention *and* praise before
it all collapses and we are all rolled into the same moist
grit clay of this earth we chug away on, breathing in
then out, our wings and tails clipped, but our eyes
and hands ready to mime this paradise before
the darkness falls.

LISTENING TO LIGHTFOOT ON THE HIGHWAY

All the way down the curved, tricky fall into the flats
of Kelowna from Vernon, wheeling around those asphalt
bends so much like music anyway, I plug a triple-CD
Lightfoot selection into the car's system and his
voice becomes another vehicle and I'm in two
falls now: the usual sleepwalking fall down
to where I work, and the other crazy fall
into my ears at sixteen, listening
to Lightfoot on his first album:
"Rich Man's Spiritual" and "The Way I
Feel" and Phil Ochs' "Changes."
As the car delivers one world all by itself,
my eyes and hands part of that world,
of course, I hit the repeat button over
and over again, listening to "Steel Rail Blues"
seven times before stopping in the parking
lot, sometimes only listening to a fragment
before going back to the beginning again
as I imagined myself, my younger self,
listening to this song for the first time
in 1966. I'm drawn into a trance
of physics allowing me to return as
a meta-consciousness surrounding that
time, something my younger self
guessed in the moment itself even,
the 'you' it always imagined
was watching, coaxing everything
along. As I turn the key off in its
ignition sleeve, I wonder what self
observes me in this instant, what music
surrounds me, some dark further grace,
some song?

Trees

We live under these trees and I guess I never believed I'd be so
overwhelmed by green and all the quirky demanding situations
these otherwise sturdy and dependable trees can get into,
didn't register them on a personal level
as my allies, didn't quite catch them on my radar. Now that I
have, I walk into the mornings transformed to meet
a new world I'd never noticed curling around
me, bucking me up, sharp indigo against
the snow, velvet in the spring,
and the endless activity
of trees, always up
to something, always
leaning into
seasons with
a surety mixed
with knowing
and a guile for
the unexpected,
strong lessons for me
so late in my
own elements,
but still
ringing, still
enfolding
myself for
and against
the wind.

Heat

Kicking around the house
staying home on purpose these days,
hiding out, fixing the fence,
mowing the lawn, sheathing
the deck so I can buy another year
before I have to replace it —
all the detritus of living
the life we live, all the stuff
that needs to be done — how
wonderful to drop my hands into
those rough old gloves or, heaven
forbid, the moist ancient dirt itself,
the musk of it, the nails and screws
and rakes and ladders and drills
and my trusty old jig-saw cutting through
3/8" plywood like butter I tell ya!
Another person in me who hides out
most of the time, ignored, springs
into action, entertained, curious,
alert for corners and angles,
for my shoes on the roof's shingles,
the angle of my foot against the sky,
the mysterious joining of things, all
these memories of man-eyes this
person knows, all the sighs
and sudden twists and breaths,
as my legs ache trying to hold
up the lattice frame while
I'm adjusting its corners with one
hand spread over the joints
and the other hand screwing in the screws,

knowing exactly what to do, how
to keep the revolutions going,
how to ignore the salt in my eyes
and simply focus on the rushing
road of the texture of everything
alive, gulping it in, gasping
to be back here once again,
balancing everything I've
become on two feeble contact
points against the keel
of the roof of my house, a maniac,
alive and well, laughing
for no reason at the crow
eyeing me from the maple
across the impossibly green
lawn, above the sprinkler
whirling redemption
over the dark cement,
all this under the black rim
of my Archibald Lampman hat
in the noonday heat, all

revolutions in tact,

revolving, spitting us out

one by one back into the earth,

our ideas just another generation

gone wrong, spun into the rich

moist soil, leaving

our best seeds there maybe,

incubating them, a design

in-tact, waiting for rain

and time and innocence:

another turn on

the wheel.

THE MARTYR

A jazz musician was once quoted as saying: "People wonder why we get paid relatively well. Man, we take people's chances for them."
— Ian Carr, *Miles Davis: The Definitive Biography* (1999)

It was the last thing, the last thing he ever imagined he'd turn into
and much like the last martyrish price paid for all his good will, his enthusiasm, his ability
to be a confidence for other people. He wasn't stupid. He knew through the long
length of what was surely self-sacrifice that everything also served his own
ends, protected him, gave him a power he must have needed or wanted, but
even so, he knew also that what he'd pulled off was as close to altruism
as you'd get in this secular field, as close as you'd come, and yet
it had overwhelmed him in the end, had created too
many things to do, too much to float, and he
could see the heavy undoing of it all
and had to simply accept it now, all its
great costumes and designs
floating down like
cinders in the air,
tatters.

He had to stand back so he could retreat into his own self again . . . a self he quite
liked and found fascinating most of the time . . . more fascinating,
in fact, than many of the selves gathering around him lately to advance
their causes. He was, in the end, bored by them, especially by their
lack of confidence and inability to work hard that lay just beneath
the swaggering self-promotion, the set speeches
about culture and regionalism etc etc cough, cough, sputter,
sputter, gasp, wheeze, chortle, *ahem!* . . .

It was only in finally announcing the high regard he had
for *himself* that he could leave these martyrish clothes behind,
twist and shuffle them off in a pile as he walked naked,
straight into the skin of his own promise
and will, unaccompanied, smiling,
sure of himself.

The Peanut Crunching Crowd

Sure, she was likely bitter, even paranoid when she hauled this
phrase down the long charcoal hallway of her poem, young Sylvia
gauging her gas bills, her kitchen, the muted light from the window
above the sink, the laughter of children in the distant cluttered
collage of morning traffic, a radio whispering in another room, dust
motes hanging like unfinished sentences in the otherwise still air, an ache
in the pit of the stomach for some kind of crowd on the one hand, some
sense of the rich fabric she'd fashioned, but against that ache, another
just for love, health, being freed from the glare of one
kind of light drawing her forward, and another light
that simply *is*: revealing the lilacs blooming before
she smells their scent, a black rook rearranging
its own order in the rain, nothing else, angels
everywhere in this light, no self-consciousness,
not random even, but her hands a web of flesh
on the cold table-top next to — *not*
a descent either — porcelain cup
of warm tea.

Watching My Students Write An Exam On Wilderness
For Don Coles

Talk about wilderness, I've created one right here myself: all
the tension, body movement, endless rustling of feet and jeans,
unseen, seen. There! No, quick! There! See? I've managed to do
these students in, reducing seventy-three adults to a childlike worry
that cannot end, ah! Such a desired, masochistic part of these top-down,
bottom-up times anyway, I can't believe I created this moment
for them, just to show them, I guess, who knows?

When I drove down the long, domesticated highway from Vernon
this morning in the rain, the 4th movement of Mahler's 5th Symphony
twisting and spiralling like smoke above my Starbuck's coffee cup
squat in its tight plastic sleeve, I laughed out loud, a pathetic Dirk
Bogarde — pancake make-up sweating down my fevered face
in the final scene of my own *Death In Venice* — when I saw Oyama's
green peninsula, that splint of lush land preventing two lakes from being
one, and there it was, that bridge again.

> *Soft this eastern, morning light, soft this music cradling*
> *my head, soft me for once, not thinking hard lines, control,*
> *dominion, grid. Give it up! Whew!*

> *And boyoboyoboyoboy! I murmured, ever hopeful, ever*
> *on it, why can't I simply be this thing I have so carefully*
> *concealed, the best part, the most unreliable but sure*
> *song I know has always been there and I can't forget*
> *this, I won't!*

Of course, I *did*, the usual, but it came back to me tonight,
sitting here watching my students, thinking of wildernesses, then
of that same highway, a night sky above it now, its cantilevered
cathedral of stars and nebulae still there, still waiting, and me
somewhere up there too, suspended over Oyama in that Bill Evans'
cobalt ruin of green and blue northern lights, that crazy sheeted
armature I've done everything to stop: me up there, a monstrance,
waiting for the sun to bleach into a safe invisibility again.

BILL EVANS AND THIS SKY TODAY

*The order you sense in cadence is more like a passage of music, or a movement of dance,
than a geometrical figure . . .*
— Dennis Lee, *Body Music: Essays* (1998)

Got me again, light trickster, shaman
of anticipation, space and the volume
of the silences between: the gap. "Sunday Nights
At The Vanguard" slipping in and out
of consciousness behind me as I sit here
marking the last of this semester's
compositions. I love to use that precise
word with them — composition —
and lob it gently back at those innocent,
faked all-knowing eyes, lost, as mine
were at the same age, in a sureness that
seems unbelievable to me looking
back at it, but which also allowed me,
as it allows them, to be lucky enough
sometimes to improvise
out of the blue, seize a small phrase
from the air and play it back at me, young
enough and sure enough not to be
obstructed by knowledge, or by
an acquired humility that moves as surely
into a soft shimmering silence
sometimes, it is so full. So I laugh
and am amazed by how it happens,

and how, like that thick grey sky
outside the window this morning —
these burnished and folding fogs
and mists closing in on the morning
hills, the late November, edgy,
stubble-strewn valley walls
drawn into a crazy improvised
trance by the creases of wind
and moisture of air just before
snow — how like that sky
these young voices close in
on me, wrap me up in promises:
Bill Evans just before
a deluge of perfectly thick
white.

Variations: brothers

For my brother, the singer, Tim Lent

Glen Gould's "Goldberg Variations" perforate the solid
darkness of the living room behind me, and I'm thinking
of you again, though we hardly seem to know one another
sometimes, you my little brother, born when I was thirteen
for Christ's sake, me the older one who went away and stayed
away, but you the one all the same I think of on certain
nights when the house is quiet and I'm not humming
in the everlasting drill of things to be done, things to be
finished, and I catch myself at rest in a block of sus-
pended darkness, delighting in music as delicate,
as sturdy, as lace-like as Gould's, at rest,
exhausted but at rest, and I see the luck in my life
and I think of you because I want you to have the same
rests, the same luck because you have the soul for them,
and the gift of singing.
                              (You must look at
me sometimes and think, shit he's got
it made for sure, that lucky fool, and I
would never blame you for thinking
that. It's true. *It's true.* But you've
got it made in another and you know it. You
and your children and the day-to-day
in the old Ritchie neighbourhood I met
Margaret Repka and Barbara Fedema
in, my crazy old high school days, David Ross
and I driving around in his father's
Pontiac, sitting at the A&W, eyeing
girls we were too young and inno-
cent to attract, hopeless

Platonists, stranded in a New
World. I love the street where you
live because part of me, more than you
even, still lives there, walks around late
at night, wondering, wondering.

                                You're standing
in the doorway of your garage. It's midnight.
You're having a smoke. You can hear the car
cooling down behind you over the distant hum
of the 99th Street traffic, strange little heaves and cracks
in the quiet, pops of coils and wires settling, the car
slouching back on its haunches in the oiled dark,
restless, sequestered. And you, the human engine, still
chuffing, still idling, standing there in the sweet dark
of another Edmonton spring night, your hands moving
the cigarette ash through the air, small red
arcs through the black.
                          They're all asleep in the house.
Occasionally, a neighbourhood cat breaks another layer
of silence, either lunging after or away from something
else that is alive that you cannot pick off or name.

They're all asleep and hopeful.

You're hopeful, too, but you know
they need you to be: you are their horizon,
everything of theirs falling forward as it's
supposed to, the weight of it on you compared
to me, those expectant eyes, wondering
and hesitant, but sure of *you* at least.

I'm standing on my back porch
in exactly the same moment, a thousand
miles away in the mountains, connected
by a mathematics of sky, some shared
coordinates in the darkness, smelling
the lilacs taking over the neighbourhood
tonight: their thick, decadent sweetness.
A night owl that has been nesting
in a Jack Pine over Groenen's garage
for three years, sutures the dark with a primeval
hoot, as if we're in this together, the two
of us. Jude is asleep far away in the centre
of the house. She doesn't know I'm standing
out here. In the old days, it would be because I
was having a smoke too, but I'm not anymore,
though I still think of its sweet oblivion all
the time. Standing here thinking
of you now, inhaling you instead.

One hundred years from now
there won't be a single soul
who remembers us, no
less thinks about what kind
of lives we led.

But here we are in this black fugue,
alive and wondering, two sets
of blue eyes staring into Eden, gauging it, wary,
hesitant, balancing one kind of natural hope
against another dark that has always held
us, a weight we cannot shake, but its
own dignity, too.

No matter the twittering
hands and lungs and eyes,
the rough texture of this ride
at times: two brothers inhaling
landscapes as air,

two skins suspended in
Gould's fire: completing
one another in a shape we
do not have the mathematics
to name.

LIGHT

I set my feet with care in such a world.
                    — *William Stafford*

Walk out into the kitchen's morning
light sifting through the half-opened
smudged window and I wonder how
do these surfaces become me
become the life I lead and lead
me on, invisible threads
in a web of ritual, a design
that's itself only half-opened
to light sometimes, always
half-hidden, too, hiding
another kind of light
in me, I suspect.

And it's when the two
fields of light collide
in a crazy sideways surprise,
when some corridor prism
rushes up through the blood
to the eyes to the mind
wrestling with itself,
and is caught turning in the other,
wilder light that these two
forests mirror one
another and all grids
and order collapse into a geometry
that cannot be envisioned
but simply, wildly, is.

You turn a faucet, you
feel the chrome handle
while another part of you
reaches for the coffee beans
and all surfaces, outside and in,
are illuminating this instant
of pure glee, pure surface,
the skin of any god you might
want to name, or any dignity
that has avoided the light
so far in the dark.

Snow

The first snow here is tricky. You have
to work to read its sides, its surfaces
and how they transform, hide, and alter
the forms of things. Only the first snows.
Afterwards, once you adjust your eyes,
you aren't so easily fooled, as if your
vision alters its physics to compen-
sate so you can reduce things
to real surfaces beneath this platonic
veneer, this guess in the dark,
in the white.

If you're a daily driver, of course,
all this becomes practical,
necessary. Last year,
on the morning of the first snow,
seventeen cars rolled
into the ditches between Vernon
and Oyama, four people
were injured and one died. I drove
past three of these accidents
on the way down in the early
morning, and past the death
in the late afternoon dusk,
a suspended time
for the eye, the scariest time
to be driving, caught between
two worlds. By the next
morning, though, given
the same amount of snow
having fallen through
the night, not one accident.

Everyone had adjusted.
We were moving through
the winter with new eyes.
That's the way it is, what
I meant to say earlier.

I talked to my mother on Sunday
afternoon. She lives in Edmonton
and has always been obsessed by weather
changes. Because I live in the interior,
in the mountains, she finds my landscape
constantly satisfying because
of its extremes, its surprises. This
summer the fires, then the floods,
now the snow. Endless variables,
lots to talk about.

She's eighty-two
and I think of her more and more
each day, the older she gets, be-
cause I do not want to lose
her yet; I do not want her
to vanish from my sight.

But once I see through
the inflation of my sense
of her caused by the chance
of her disappearance, I'm fine.
I know beneath all this
movement, there is
the ground she is.

This morning, in the first
snow we've had this fall,
I pull in behind a Chevy Van
whose logic I can read
and trust. And while the crazy
boneheads in the half-tons
race over the snow and
black ice, their necks leaning
into cell phones as they
jack-knife through the curves
passing us, my eyes hold the road
and see through a Byzantium
of white to what lies beneath it,
what is always waiting
at the end of seeing.

Thinking of First Meeting Don Coles in 1971

Rain sheeted afternoons followed by coiling fog, the silvered
backs of mirrors, thumbed pages of Cheevers, some obscure
scene from Updike, an east-coast town maybe, buried in heavy
shade-dappled elms, some young man, say, a recently-graduated
professor, arrives to teach at the local college. First year English
Literature. Sure. That'll work. As he's unpacking his small
used car on the side-street, eyeing the window of his fourth-floor flat
from the pavement below, reaching into the trunk in a sudden sigh
for something, a young woman spies him from the bakery across
the street, smiles that wry, never-stated understanding only the
young *can* smile, that endless math of conjoining,
and he winks back at her and feels the weight of the Dunlop
Tennis Racquet in his right hand, then his thin wallet in his jeans,
the pin-stripe on his tab-down cotton collar chafing his skin, his
future *in* this moment as he knew it would always be like this:
each moment another future, another history, forgotten as she
reaches for a tray behind her and he mounts the rough, oil-
stained and atomistic stairs to reassume the usual.

That's who you reminded me of when I first met you: the sly
East-coast and easy elegance contained in that wink,
the creaking mirror of its whole tableau, its grace and silvered
open-endedness: the confidence I'd never have myself.

Winter Blues

Have to get all this sand and dust rinsed
off my territory, scrape it raw for the rain
and the sun, open it up to the seeds
and the yawn of green that almost makes
you pass out, gives you a fever,
forces you to your knees.

Every year, the same old thing, walking
my way out of winter, down the long
streets where I can become so lost I
need a map of some kind to find my
way out of these crazy corners
and blind alleys and mammoth
black buildings and factories
I cannot even recognize
or name, like waking up
I guess, but shit, not
from some great
dream I can tell
you that!

You don't have to be Tim
Lilburn to realise this is serious,
this turning sideways
on the earth into another season,

another world even, that's what it feels
like, where the heart can lose
its dark winter roots, the way
it has buried itself in all
the ground cover, the snow
and wind, free itself from all
that intricate, necessary dark
in order, as it seems to know
how to do every year, break
through to the light.

DOG IN A HALF-TON SUN

Nose in the air snuffling it in
gulping the breeze, spittle flying away
in streaks against the indigo
of the truck's cab.

Sniffing around, pausing a bit,
a show of restlessness
for an imagined audience — either
the dog's owner sitting
in a chair somewhere,
or a menace in this otherwise
flat and normal dusk, full
of the goodwill of sun
and the smell of coffee brewing
in this small café bending into
the early evening like a shovel
into sand near water: all weight
and enamel, lifting, glistening
this gesture into early evening.

The dog at the gates of it.

Me at the heart of it.

An indecipherable maze.

A myth unfolding

as story: but new story, new

myth, *new beings.*

John Lent has been publishing poetry, fiction, and non-fiction nationally and internationally for the past thirty years. His work has appeared in various literary journals including *Matrix*, *This Magazine*, *Grain*, and *The Malahat Review*. He recently published a book of conversations with Robert Kroetsch about the writing life (*Abundance*, Kalamalka Press). Lent's last novel, *So It Won't Go Away* (Thistledown Press), was short-listed for a 2005 BC Book Prize. In his thirty-year writing career, Lent has presented his work across Canada, in the United States, and in numerous Western European countries. He is one of the founders of Kalamalka Press and the Kalamalka Institute for Working Writers, and currently serves as the Regional Dean at North Okanagan College. Lent lives in Vernon, BC, with his wife, artist Jude Clarke, and plays in The Lent/Fraser/Wall Trio, a jazz and roots group.